EMMANUEL JOSEPH

Taste of the Future, Exploring Food, Society, and the Rise of Robotic Chefs

Copyright © 2025 by Emmanuel Joseph

All rights reserved. No part of this publication may be reproduced, stored or transmitted in any form or by any means, electronic, mechanical, photocopying, recording, scanning, or otherwise without written permission from the publisher. It is illegal to copy this book, post it to a website, or distribute it by any other means without permission.

First edition

This book was professionally typeset on Reedsy.
Find out more at reedsy.com

Contents

1	Chapter 1: A Culinary Revolution Unfolds	1
2	Chapter 2: The Origins of Robotic Chefs	3
3	Chapter 3: The Science Behind Robotic Cooking	5
4	Chapter 4: The Cultural Impact of Robotic Chefs	7
5	Chapter 5: The Ethics of Automated Cooking	9
6	Chapter 6: The Future of Culinary Education	11
7	Chapter 7: Robotic Chefs in Restaurants	13
8	Chapter 8: The Home Kitchen Revolution	15
9	Chapter 9: The Role of AI in Culinary Innovation	17
10	Chapter 10: The Impact on Food Culture	19
11	Chapter 11: The Future of Dining	21
12	Chapter 12: Embracing the Culinary Future	23
13	Chapter 13: Robotic Chefs in Space	25
14	Chapter 14: The Economics of Robotic Chefs	27
15	Chapter 15: The Role of Robotic Chefs in Healthcare	29
16	Chapter 16: Robotic Chefs in Education and Training	31
17	Chapter 17: The Global Impact of Robotic Chefs	33
18	Chapter 18: The Environmental Impact of Robotic Chefs	35
19	Chapter 19: The Intersection of Robotics and Culinary Arts	37
20	Chapter 20: The Social Implications of Robotic Chefs	39
21	Chapter 21: The Future of Culinary Creativity	41
22	Chapter 22: The Legacy of Robotic Chefs	43

1

Chapter 1: A Culinary Revolution Unfolds

In recent years, the culinary world has witnessed a remarkable transformation with the emergence of robotic chefs. These cutting-edge machines, equipped with state-of-the-art technology and artificial intelligence, are revolutionizing how we prepare and consume food. Gone are the days when cooking was solely a human endeavor; robotic chefs are now taking center stage in kitchens across the globe. As we delve into the fascinating journey of this culinary revolution, it becomes clear that these mechanical marvels are not just gadgets but harbingers of a new era in gastronomy.

The allure of robotic chefs lies in their precision and efficiency. Unlike human cooks, they can replicate recipes with unwavering consistency, ensuring that every dish is prepared to perfection. This level of precision has opened up new possibilities for experimentation and innovation in the kitchen. From molecular gastronomy to intricate pastry designs, robotic chefs are pushing the boundaries of what is possible, creating dishes that were once the stuff of dreams. The culinary landscape is evolving, and robotic chefs are at the forefront of this transformation.

Moreover, the rise of robotic chefs is not just about convenience; it also addresses some of the pressing challenges faced by the food industry. With an increasing demand for sustainable and ethically sourced ingredients, robotic chefs can help optimize resource usage and reduce waste. By meticulously measuring and portioning ingredients, these machines ensure that nothing goes to waste. This shift towards more sustainable practices is a crucial step in addressing the global food crisis and ensuring a more equitable distribution of resources.

As we embark on this journey to explore the impact of robotic chefs on society, it is essential to consider the broader implications. The integration of technology into our culinary traditions raises questions about the role of human creativity and intuition in the kitchen. While robotic chefs excel in precision, they lack the emotional connection and intuition that human cooks bring to their creations. This dynamic interplay between technology and tradition will shape the future of food and society.

2

Chapter 2: The Origins of Robotic Chefs

The concept of robotic chefs may seem like a recent innovation, but its roots can be traced back to the early days of automation and artificial intelligence. The idea of using machines to assist in cooking dates back to the mid-20th century when the first automated kitchen appliances were introduced. These early devices, such as electric mixers and coffee makers, paved the way for more sophisticated culinary robots. The journey from simple machines to fully functional robotic chefs has been marked by significant technological advancements and visionary thinking.

The development of robotic chefs gained momentum in the late 20th and early 21st centuries with the advent of advanced robotics and AI. Researchers and engineers began to explore the possibilities of creating machines that could mimic human cooking techniques. The breakthrough came with the integration of machine learning algorithms, which enabled robotic chefs to learn and adapt to different cooking styles. These algorithms allowed machines to analyze vast amounts of culinary data and replicate complex recipes with remarkable accuracy.

One of the pioneering projects in the field of robotic chefs was the creation of Moley Robotics' kitchen robot in 2015. This groundbreaking invention featured a pair of robotic arms that could perform intricate cooking tasks, from chopping vegetables to plating dishes. The robot's ability to mimic the movements of a human chef opened up new possibilities for automation in the kitchen. Since then, several other companies and research institutions have joined the race to develop more advanced and versatile robotic chefs.

As the technology behind robotic chefs continues to evolve, so does their potential impact on the culinary world. The integration of sensors, cameras, and AI-driven algorithms allows these machines to adapt to different cooking environments and learn from their experiences. This continuous improvement in their capabilities ensures that robotic chefs are not just static machines but dynamic entities that can grow and evolve. The journey from concept to reality has been long and arduous, but the future of robotic chefs looks brighter than ever.

3

Chapter 3: The Science Behind Robotic Cooking

At the heart of every robotic chef lies a complex web of technology and innovation. The science behind robotic cooking involves a harmonious blend of robotics, artificial intelligence, and culinary expertise. To understand how these machines operate, it is essential to delve into the key components that make robotic chefs so efficient and precise. From advanced sensors to sophisticated algorithms, every element plays a crucial role in transforming raw ingredients into delectable dishes.

One of the fundamental aspects of robotic cooking is the use of sensors and cameras. These devices allow robotic chefs to perceive their environment and interact with ingredients in real-time. For instance, high-resolution cameras can identify the shape, size, and color of ingredients, enabling the robot to make precise cuts and measurements. Additionally, temperature sensors ensure that food is cooked to perfection, eliminating the risk of undercooking or overcooking.

Another critical component of robotic chefs is the artificial intelligence algorithms that power their decision-making processes. Machine learning enables these robots to analyze vast amounts of culinary data and learn from their experiences. By studying recipes, cooking techniques, and even customer preferences, robotic chefs can continuously improve their performance. This adaptive learning process allows them to replicate complex dishes with remarkable accuracy and consistency.

The mechanical design of robotic chefs is also a marvel of engineering. These machines are equipped with robotic arms and hands that can perform intricate tasks with precision. The dexterity of these robotic limbs allows them to handle delicate ingredients and perform tasks that require a high degree of skill. Moreover, the integration of advanced motors and actuators ensures that the movements of the robotic chef are smooth and controlled. This seamless coordination between hardware and software is what makes robotic cooking a reality.

4

Chapter 4: The Cultural Impact of Robotic Chefs

The rise of robotic chefs is not just a technological phenomenon; it also has profound cultural implications. As these machines become more prevalent in kitchens around the world, they are reshaping our relationship with food and dining. The cultural impact of robotic chefs extends beyond the realm of gastronomy, influencing our social interactions, traditions, and even our perceptions of creativity and craftsmanship.

One of the most significant cultural shifts brought about by robotic chefs is the democratization of gourmet cooking. With these machines, anyone can prepare restaurant-quality meals in the comfort of their own home. This accessibility to high-quality food has the potential to change the way we think about cooking and dining. No longer limited to professional chefs, gourmet cooking is becoming a shared experience that transcends social and economic barriers.

Moreover, the integration of robotic chefs into our culinary traditions raises questions about the preservation of cultural heritage. Cooking is often seen as a form of artistic expression, deeply rooted in cultural identity and history. The use of robotic chefs challenges the notion of authenticity and tradition in the kitchen. While these machines can replicate recipes with precision, they lack the human touch and intuition that characterize traditional cooking. This tension between technology and tradition will shape the future of culinary practices.

The cultural impact of robotic chefs also extends to the dining experience itself. In a world where convenience and efficiency are highly valued, robotic chefs offer a new way of experiencing food. Automated kitchens and AI-driven dining experiences are becoming increasingly popular in restaurants and homes. This shift towards automation has the potential to redefine our social interactions around food. The act of sharing a meal, once a deeply communal activity, is being transformed by the presence of robotic chefs.

As we navigate the cultural landscape shaped by robotic chefs, it is essential to consider the broader implications for society. The integration of technology into our culinary traditions challenges our perceptions of creativity, craftsmanship, and authenticity. While robotic chefs offer exciting possibilities for innovation and experimentation, they also raise questions about the role of human intuition and emotion in the kitchen. The cultural impact of robotic chefs is a complex and multifaceted phenomenon that will continue to evolve in the coming years.

5

Chapter 5: The Ethics of Automated Cooking

The rise of robotic chefs also brings ethical considerations to the forefront. As these machines become more integrated into our culinary practices, it is essential to examine the ethical implications of automated cooking. From concerns about job displacement to questions about privacy and data security, the ethics of robotic chefs is a topic that warrants careful consideration.

One of the most pressing ethical concerns is the potential impact on employment in the food industry. The automation of cooking processes has the potential to displace human workers, particularly in roles that involve repetitive tasks. While robotic chefs can increase efficiency and reduce costs, they also raise questions about the future of jobs in the culinary sector. It is crucial to find a balance between embracing technological advancements and ensuring that human workers are not left behind.

Privacy and data security are also important ethical considerations in the context of robotic chefs. These machines often rely on vast amounts of data to improve their performance and adapt to user preferences. This data can include personal information about users' dietary habits, preferences, and even health conditions. It is essential to ensure that this data is collected, stored, and used responsibly, with robust safeguards in place to protect users' privacy.

Moreover, the ethical implications of robotic chefs extend to issues of sustainability and resource usage. While these machines can optimize ingredient usage and reduce waste, they also have an environmental footprint. The production, maintenance, and disposal of robotic chefs involve the use of resources and energy. It is important to consider the environmental impact of these machines and explore ways to mitigate their carbon footprint.

The ethics of automated cooking also encompass questions about the role of technology in our culinary traditions. As robotic chefs become more prevalent, there is a risk of losing the human touch and emotional connection that characterize traditional cooking. It is essential to strike a balance between embracing technological advancements and preserving the cultural and emotional aspects of cooking. The ethical considerations of robotic chefs are complex and multifaceted, requiring ongoing dialogue and reflection.

6

Chapter 6: The Future of Culinary Education

The rise of robotic chefs is also transforming the landscape of culinary education. As these machines become more integrated into professional kitchens, culinary schools and training programs are adapting to prepare the next generation of chefs for a future where technology plays a central role. The future of culinary education is being shaped by the need to equip aspiring chefs with the skills and knowledge being shaped by the need to equip aspiring chefs with the skills and knowledge to work alongside robotic counterparts. This shift in culinary education is not just about learning to operate machines but also about understanding the potential of technology to enhance creativity and innovation in the kitchen.

One of the key areas of focus in the future of culinary education is the integration of technology into traditional cooking techniques. Aspiring chefs are being trained to work with robotic chefs, understanding how to program and interact with these machines to achieve the desired results. This involves not only technical skills but also a deep understanding of the principles of robotics and artificial intelligence. By bridging the gap between technology and culinary arts, future chefs will be well-equipped to navigate the evolving landscape of the food industry.

Moreover, culinary education is placing a greater emphasis on sustainability and resource management. With the help of robotic chefs, students are learning to optimize ingredient usage and reduce waste. This focus on sustainability is essential in addressing the global food crisis and ensuring a more equitable distribution of resources. By incorporating these principles into their training, aspiring chefs are being prepared to make a positive impact on the world through their culinary practices.

Another important aspect of the future of culinary education is the emphasis on creativity and innovation. While robotic chefs excel in precision and efficiency, human chefs bring a unique touch of creativity and intuition to the kitchen. Culinary schools are fostering an environment where students can experiment with new flavors, techniques, and presentation styles. By encouraging creativity and innovation, culinary education is ensuring that the next generation of chefs can push the boundaries of what is possible in the kitchen.

As we look to the future of culinary education, it is clear that the integration of technology and tradition will play a crucial role. By embracing the potential of robotic chefs while preserving the essence of human creativity and craftsmanship, the culinary world is poised for a new era of innovation and excellence.

7

Chapter 7: Robotic Chefs in Restaurants

The integration of robotic chefs into restaurants is revolutionizing the dining experience. These machines are not just confined to home kitchens; they are making their way into professional kitchens, transforming the way food is prepared and served. The presence of robotic chefs in restaurants is changing the dynamics of the culinary industry, offering new possibilities for efficiency, consistency, and innovation.

One of the most significant advantages of robotic chefs in restaurants is their ability to streamline operations. These machines can perform repetitive tasks with precision and speed, allowing human chefs to focus on more creative and complex aspects of cooking. By automating routine tasks such as chopping, mixing, and plating, robotic chefs can reduce the workload of kitchen staff and improve overall efficiency. This not only enhances the dining experience for customers but also reduces the stress and strain on human chefs.

Moreover, robotic chefs in restaurants offer unparalleled consistency in food preparation. Unlike human chefs, who may vary in their techniques and execution, robotic chefs can replicate recipes with exact precision every time. This level of consistency is particularly valuable in fast-paced restaurant environments where maintaining quality and uniformity is crucial. Customers can expect the same high standard of food with every visit, ensuring a reliable and enjoyable dining experience.

The presence of robotic chefs in restaurants also opens up new possibilities for culinary innovation. These machines can experiment with new techniques, ingredients, and presentation styles that may be challenging for human chefs to achieve. For instance, robotic chefs can execute intricate molecular gastronomy techniques with precision, creating visually stunning and innovative dishes. By pushing the boundaries of what is possible in the kitchen, robotic chefs are driving culinary creativity to new heights.

As robotic chefs become more prevalent in restaurants, it is essential to consider the broader implications for the industry. The integration of these machines raises questions about the role of human chefs and the preservation of culinary traditions. While robotic chefs offer numerous benefits, it is crucial to strike a balance between automation and the human touch that defines the culinary experience. The future of dining will be shaped by the harmonious coexistence of technology and tradition.

8

Chapter 8: The Home Kitchen Revolution

The impact of robotic chefs is not limited to professional kitchens; they are also transforming home cooking. With the advent of advanced robotic appliances, home kitchens are becoming more sophisticated and efficient. The presence of robotic chefs in home kitchens is revolutionizing the way we cook and dine, making gourmet cooking accessible to everyone.

One of the most significant advantages of robotic chefs in home kitchens is the convenience they offer. These machines can handle time-consuming and labor-intensive tasks, such as chopping, mixing, and cooking, allowing home cooks to focus on other aspects of meal preparation. By automating routine tasks, robotic chefs can save time and effort, making cooking more enjoyable and stress-free.

Moreover, robotic chefs in home kitchens offer unparalleled precision and consistency. These machines can replicate recipes with exact accuracy, ensuring that every dish is prepared to perfection. This level of precision is particularly valuable for home cooks who may not have the same level of expertise as professional chefs. With the help of robotic chefs, anyone can create restaurant-quality meals in their own kitchen.

The presence of robotic chefs in home kitchens also opens up new possibilities for culinary experimentation. These machines can execute complex techniques and recipes that may be challenging for home cooks to achieve. For instance, robotic chefs can perform intricate pastry designs or execute precise cooking techniques, such as sous-vide, with ease. By pushing the boundaries of home cooking, robotic chefs are empowering home cooks to explore new flavors and techniques.

As robotic chefs become more prevalent in home kitchens, it is essential to consider the broader implications for our relationship with food. The integration of these machines raises questions about the role of human intuition and creativity in cooking. While robotic chefs offer numerous benefits, it is crucial to preserve the emotional connection and joy that come from preparing and sharing a meal. The future of home cooking will be shaped by the harmonious coexistence of technology and tradition.

9

Chapter 9: The Role of AI in Culinary Innovation

The rise of robotic chefs is closely tied to the advancements in artificial intelligence (AI) and machine learning. AI plays a central role in the development and operation of these machines, enabling them to replicate complex cooking techniques and adapt to different culinary environments. The integration of AI in culinary practices is driving innovation and transforming the way we think about food.

One of the key areas where AI is making a significant impact is in recipe development. Machine learning algorithms can analyze vast amounts of culinary data, including recipes, ingredients, and cooking techniques. By identifying patterns and trends, AI can generate new and innovative recipes that push the boundaries of traditional cooking. This ability to experiment with new flavors and combinations is opening up exciting possibilities for culinary creativity.

Moreover, AI is enhancing the precision and efficiency of robotic chefs. These machines rely on AI algorithms to make real-time decisions and adjustments during the cooking process. For instance, temperature sensors and cameras provide valuable data that AI can use to ensure that food is cooked to perfection. This level of precision is particularly valuable in complex cooking techniques, such as molecular gastronomy, where even the slightest deviation can affect the final outcome.

The integration of AI in culinary practices is also driving sustainability and resource optimization. Machine learning algorithms can analyze data on ingredient usage, waste, and energy consumption to identify areas for improvement. By optimizing resource usage, AI can help reduce waste and minimize the environmental impact of cooking. This focus on sustainability is essential in addressing the global food crisis and ensuring a more equitable distribution of resources.

As we explore the role of AI in culinary innovation, it is essential to consider the broader implications for the food industry. The integration of AI raises questions about the role of human creativity and intuition in cooking. While AI can enhance precision and efficiency, it is crucial to preserve the emotional connection and artistry that characterize traditional cooking. The future of culinary innovation will be shaped by the harmonious coexistence of technology and human creativity.

10

Chapter 10: The Impact on Food Culture

The rise of robotic chefs and the integration of technology into culinary practices are having a profound impact on food culture. As these machines become more prevalent, they are reshaping our relationship with food, dining, and culinary traditions. The impact on food culture extends beyond the realm of gastronomy, influencing our social interactions, traditions, and even our perceptions of creativity and craftsmanship.

One of the most significant cultural shifts brought about by robotic chefs is the democratization of gourmet cooking. With these machines, anyone can prepare restaurant-quality meals in the comfort of their own home. This accessibility to high-quality food has the potential to change the way we think about cooking and dining. No longer limited to professional chefs, gourmet cooking is becoming a shared experience that transcends social and economic barriers.

Moreover, the integration of robotic chefs into our culinary traditions raises questions about the preservation of cultural heritage. Cooking is often seen as a form of artistic expression, deeply rooted in cultural identity and history. The use of robotic chefs challenges the notion of authenticity and tradition in the kitchen. While these machines can replicate recipes with precision, they lack the human touch and intuition that characterize traditional cooking. This tension between technology and tradition will shape the future of culinary practices.

The impact of robotic chefs on food culture also extends to the dining experience itself. In a world where convenience and efficiency are highly valued, robotic chefs offer a new way of experiencing food. Automated kitchens and AI-driven dining experiences are becoming increasingly popular in restaurants and homes. This shift towards automation has the potential to redefine our social interactions around food. The act of sharing a meal, once a deeply communal activity, is being transformed by the presence of robotic chefs.

As we navigate the cultural landscape shaped by robotic chefs, it is essential to consider the broader implications for society. The integration of technology into our culinary traditions challenges our perceptions of creativity, craftsmanship, and authenticity. While robotic chefs offer exciting possibilities for innovation and experimentation, they also raise questions about the role of human intuition and emotion in the kitchen. The impact of robotic chefs on food culture is a complex and multifaceted phenomenon that will continue to evolve in the coming years.

11

Chapter 11: The Future of Dining

The rise of robotic chefs is transforming the future of dining, offering new possibilities for culinary experiences experiences that blend technology with culinary artistry. The future of dining will be defined by the seamless integration of robotic chefs, AI-driven systems, and human creativity, offering a dynamic and personalized experience for every diner.

One of the most exciting aspects of the future of dining is the potential for personalized culinary experiences. With the help of AI and machine learning, robotic chefs can analyze individual preferences and dietary needs to create customized dishes tailored to each diner's taste. This level of personalization goes beyond traditional dining, offering a unique experience that caters to the specific desires and requirements of every customer. Whether it's a health-conscious meal plan or an indulgent gourmet feast, robotic chefs can create dishes that perfectly align with each diner's preferences.

Moreover, the future of dining will be characterized by the fusion of technology and culinary artistry. Robotic chefs, equipped with advanced sensors and precision tools, can execute complex techniques and presentation styles that were once the domain of skilled human chefs. This fusion of technology and artistry opens up new possibilities for culinary innovation, allowing chefs to experiment with bold flavors, intricate designs, and cutting-edge cooking methods. The result is a dining experience that is not only delicious but also visually stunning and intellectually stimulating.

The rise of robotic chefs also has the potential to revolutionize the restaurant industry. Automated kitchens can streamline operations, reduce costs, and improve efficiency, allowing restaurants to focus on delivering exceptional service and unique experiences. This shift towards automation can also enhance food safety and hygiene, as robotic chefs can operate in controlled environments with minimal human intervention. The future of dining will be defined by the harmonious coexistence of human and robotic chefs, each bringing their unique strengths to the table.

As we look to the future of dining, it is essential to consider the broader implications for society. The integration of technology into our culinary practices raises questions about the role of human creativity, tradition, and emotion in the dining experience. While robotic chefs offer numerous benefits, it is crucial to strike a balance between automation and the human touch that defines the essence of dining. The future of dining will be shaped by the dynamic interplay between technology and tradition, offering a new and exciting culinary landscape for generations to come.

12

Chapter 12: Embracing the Culinary Future

As we conclude our exploration of the rise of robotic chefs and their impact on food, society, and the culinary world, it is clear that we are on the brink of a new era in gastronomy. The integration of technology into our culinary practices offers exciting possibilities for innovation, efficiency, and personalization. However, it also raises important questions about the role of tradition, creativity, and human intuition in the kitchen.

The future of food is not just about embracing technological advancements but also about finding a balance between innovation and tradition. Robotic chefs offer unparalleled precision and efficiency, but they lack the emotional connection and intuition that human chefs bring to their creations. As we move forward, it is essential to preserve the cultural and emotional aspects of cooking while embracing the potential of technology to enhance our culinary experiences.

Moreover, the rise of robotic chefs presents an opportunity to address some of the pressing challenges faced by the food industry. From sustainability and resource optimization to food safety and accessibility, these machines have the potential to make a positive impact on the world. By harnessing the power of technology, we can create a more equitable and sustainable food system that benefits everyone.

As we embrace the culinary future, it is essential to remain mindful of the ethical considerations and broader implications of our choices. The integration of robotic chefs into our culinary practices challenges our perceptions of creativity, craftsmanship, and authenticity. By fostering a dialogue and reflection on these issues, we can ensure that the future of food is shaped by a thoughtful and inclusive approach.

The journey of exploring the rise of robotic chefs and their impact on food, society, and the culinary world has been a fascinating one. As we look to the future, it is clear that the dynamic interplay between technology and tradition will shape the culinary landscape in new and exciting ways. By embracing the potential of robotic chefs while preserving the essence of human creativity and emotion, we can create a future where food is not just a necessity but a celebration of innovation, culture, and connection.

13

Chapter 13: Robotic Chefs in Space

As humanity sets its sights on space exploration and the colonization of other planets, the role of robotic chefs becomes increasingly significant. In the harsh and isolated environments of space, these machines can provide astronauts with nutritious and comforting meals, enhancing their overall well-being and performance. The development of robotic chefs for space missions involves unique challenges and opportunities, pushing the boundaries of culinary innovation beyond our planet.

One of the primary challenges of cooking in space is the limited availability of fresh ingredients. Robotic chefs can help address this issue by utilizing advanced preservation techniques and efficient resource management. These machines can rehydrate and prepare pre-packaged meals with precision, ensuring that astronauts receive the necessary nutrients for their long-duration missions. Additionally, robotic chefs can experiment with growing and cooking fresh produce in controlled environments, further expanding the possibilities for space cuisine.

The presence of robotic chefs in space missions also has the potential to enhance the psychological well-being of astronauts. The act of preparing and sharing a meal can provide a sense of comfort and normalcy in the isolated and stressful conditions of space. Robotic chefs can replicate familiar dishes and create new culinary experiences, offering astronauts a taste of home and a connection to their cultural heritage. This emotional support is crucial for maintaining morale and mental health during long-duration missions.

As we explore the potential of robotic chefs in space, it is essential to consider the broader implications for future space exploration. The integration of these machines into space missions represents a significant step towards creating sustainable and self-sufficient living environments beyond Earth. By harnessing the power of robotic chefs, we can ensure that astronauts have access to high-quality meals, even in the most challenging conditions. The future of space exploration will be shaped by the innovative and adaptive capabilities of robotic chefs.

14

Chapter 14: The Economics of Robotic Chefs

The rise of robotic chefs is not only transforming the culinary world but also having a significant impact on the economics of the food industry. The integration of these machines into kitchens and restaurants presents new opportunities and challenges for businesses, shaping the economic landscape of the culinary sector. Understanding the economic implications of robotic chefs is essential for navigating the evolving food industry and making informed decisions.

One of the most significant economic benefits of robotic chefs is the potential for cost savings. By automating repetitive and labor-intensive tasks, these machines can reduce the need for human labor, leading to lower operational costs for businesses. This reduction in labor costs can be particularly valuable for restaurants and food service establishments, where margins are often slim. Additionally, robotic chefs can increase efficiency and productivity, further enhancing the profitability of businesses in the food industry.

Moreover, the integration of robotic chefs into the food industry can drive innovation and create new revenue streams. These machines can experiment with new recipes, techniques, and presentation styles, offering unique culinary experiences that attract customers. By differentiating themselves through innovation, businesses can gain a competitive edge and tap into new markets. The potential for personalized dining experiences, powered by AI and machine learning, also opens up new opportunities for revenue generation.

However, the economic impact of robotic chefs is not without challenges. The initial investment in these machines can be substantial, requiring businesses to carefully consider the cost-benefit analysis. Additionally, the integration of robotic chefs may lead to job displacement, raising concerns about the future of employment in the food industry. It is essential to find a balance between embracing technological advancements and ensuring that human workers are not left behind. This balance will be crucial for creating a sustainable and inclusive economic future for the culinary sector.

As we navigate the economic landscape shaped by robotic chefs, it is essential to consider the broader implications for the food industry. The integration of these machines offers exciting possibilities for cost savings, innovation, and revenue generation. However, it also raises important questions about the future of employment and the need for a balanced approach. By understanding the economic impact of robotic chefs, we can make informed decisions that benefit businesses, workers, and consumers alike.

15

Chapter 15: The Role of Robotic Chefs in Healthcare

The integration of robotic chefs into the healthcare sector has the potential to revolutionize the way we approach nutrition and patient care. These machines can play a significant role in enhancing the quality of meals provided in hospitals, nursing homes, and other healthcare facilities. By leveraging the precision and efficiency of robotic chefs, healthcare providers can ensure that patients receive nutritious, safe, and delicious meals tailored to their specific dietary needs.

One of the primary benefits of robotic chefs in healthcare is their ability to create personalized meals for patients with specific dietary requirements. Whether it's preparing low-sodium meals for patients with hypertension or gluten-free options for those with celiac disease, robotic chefs can customize dishes with precision. By analyzing individual dietary needs and preferences, these machines can create meals that meet the nutritional requirements of each patient, contributing to their overall health and well-being.

Moreover, robotic chefs can enhance food safety and hygiene in healthcare facilities. These machines can operate in controlled environments, minimizing the risk of contamination and ensuring that food is prepared under strict sanitary conditions. This is particularly important in healthcare settings, where patients may have compromised immune systems and are more susceptible to foodborne illnesses. The precision and consistency of robotic chefs can help maintain high standards of food safety, reducing the risk of infections and complications.

The presence of robotic chefs in healthcare facilities also has the potential to improve the overall dining experience for patients. By offering a variety of delicious and visually appealing meals, these machines can enhance the enjoyment and satisfaction of patients during their stay. The act of enjoying a well-prepared meal can provide comfort and a sense of normalcy, contributing to the emotional and psychological well-being of patients. This holistic approach to patient care recognizes the importance of nutrition and dining experience in the healing process.

As we explore the role of robotic chefs in healthcare, it is essential to consider the broader implications for patient care and nutrition. The integration of these machines offers exciting possibilities for personalized nutrition, food safety, and enhanced dining experiences. By leveraging the capabilities of robotic chefs, healthcare providers can ensure that patients receive high-quality, nutritious, and enjoyable meals, contributing to their overall health and recovery.

16

Chapter 16: Robotic Chefs in Education and Training

The rise of robotic chefs is also transforming the landscape of education and training in the culinary arts. As these machines become more integrated into professional kitchens and culinary schools, they are shaping the way aspiring chefs are trained and prepared for their careers. The integration of robotic chefs into culinary education offers new opportunities for learning, experimentation, and innovation.

One of the key areas of focus in culinary education is the hands-on experience of working with robotic chefs. Aspiring chefs are being trained to operate and interact with these machines, understanding their capabilities and limitations. This involves not only technical skills but also a deep understanding of the principles of robotics and artificial intelligence. By gaining experience with robotic chefs, students are better prepared to navigate the evolving landscape of the food industry and work alongside their robotic counterparts.

Moreover, the integration of robotic chefs into culinary education fosters a culture of experimentation and innovation. These machines can perform complex techniques and replicate recipes with precision, allowing students to explore new flavors, presentation styles, and cooking methods. This environment of creativity and innovation encourages aspiring chefs to push the boundaries of traditional cooking and develop their unique culinary identities. By embracing the potential of robotic chefs, culinary schools are preparing students for a future where technology and creativity go hand in hand.

The presence of robotic chefs in culinary education also offers opportunities for collaboration and interdisciplinary learning. Students can work with experts in robotics, AI, and food science to develop new techniques and innovations in the kitchen. This interdisciplinary approach fosters a holistic understanding of the culinary arts, where technology and tradition coexist and complement each other. By promoting collaboration and cross-disciplinary learning, culinary education is preparing the next generation of chefs to lead the way in culinary innovation.

As we look to the future of culinary education, it is clear that the integration of robotic chefs will play a crucial role. By embracing the potential of these machines, culinary schools can offer students new opportunities for learning, experimentation, and innovation. The future of culinary education will be defined by the dynamic interplay between technology and creativity, preparing aspiring chefs for a future where robotic chefs are an integral part of the culinary landscape.

17

Chapter 17: The Global Impact of Robotic Chefs

The rise of robotic chefs is not limited to any one region or country; it is a global phenomenon that is transforming the culinary world across the globe. As these machines become more prevalent in kitchens and restaurants worldwide, they are having a significant impact on food culture, dining experiences, and culinary traditions in diverse regions. Understanding the global impact of robotic chefs is essential for appreciating the broader implications of this technological revolution.

One of the key areas where robotic chefs are making an impact is in the accessibility of gourmet cooking. In regions where access to high-quality ingredients and culinary expertise may be limited, these machines can democratize gourmet dining. Robotic chefs can replicate complex recipes with precision, allowing people in different parts of the world to experience dishes that were once the domain of high-end restaurants. This accessibility to gourmet cooking is transforming the way people think about food and dining, breaking down barriers and creating new opportunities for culinary exploration.

Moreover, the integration of robotic chefs into diverse culinary traditions raises questions about the preservation of cultural heritage. Cooking is often seen as a form of artistic expression, deeply rooted in cultural identity and history. The use of robotic chefs challenges the notion of authenticity and tradition in the kitchen. While these machines can replicate recipes with precision, they lack the human touch and intuition that characterize traditional cooking. This tension between technology and tradition will shape the future of culinary practices in different regions.

The global impact of robotic chefs also extends to the dining experience itself. In a world where convenience and efficiency are highly valued, robotic chefs offer a new way of experiencing food. Automated kitchens and AI-driven dining experiences are becoming increasingly popular in restaurants and homes around the world. This shift towards automation has the potential to redefine social interactions around food, creating new opportunities for connection and engagement. The act of sharing a meal, once a deeply communal activity, is being transformed by the presence of robotic chefs.

As we explore the global impact of robotic chefs, it is essential to consider the broader implications for food culture and traditions. The integration of technology into our culinary practices challenges our perceptions of creativity, craftsmanship, and authenticity. While robotic chefs offer exciting possibilities for innovation and experimentation, they also raise questions about the role of human intuition and emotion in the kitchen. The global impact of robotic chefs is a complex and multifaceted phenomenon that will continue to evolve in the coming years.

18

Chapter 18: The Environmental Impact of Robotic Chefs

The rise of robotic chefs also has significant implications for the environment. As these machines become more prevalent in kitchens and restaurants, it is essential to consider their environmental footprint and the potential for sustainability. The environmental impact of robotic chefs involves both challenges and opportunities, shaping the future of sustainable culinary practices.

One of the primary environmental benefits of robotic chefs is their ability to optimize ingredient usage and reduce waste. These machines can measure and portion ingredients with precision, ensuring that nothing goes to waste. By minimizing food waste, robotic chefs can contribute to more sustainable culinary practices and reduce the overall environmental impact of cooking. This focus on sustainability is essential in addressing the global food crisis and ensuring a more equitable distribution of resources.

Moreover, robotic chefs can enhance energy efficiency in the kitchen. These machines can operate with precision and consistency, reducing the need for energy-intensive cooking methods. For instance, robotic chefs can optimize cooking times and temperatures to minimize energy consumption. Additionally, the integration of renewable energy sources, such as solar power, into robotic kitchen systems can further reduce their environmental footprint. By promoting energy efficiency, robotic chefs can contribute to a more sustainable culinary future.

However, the environmental impact of robotic chefs is not without challenges. The production, maintenance, and disposal of these machines involve the use of resources and energy. It is essential to consider the environmental footprint of the entire lifecycle of robotic chefs, from manufacturing to end-of-life disposal. By exploring sustainable materials and recycling options, we can mitigate the environmental impact of these machines and promote a circular economy.

As we navigate the environmental landscape shaped by robotic chefs, it is essential to consider the broader implications for sustainability. The integration of these machines offers exciting possibilities for reducing waste and enhancing energy efficiency. However, it also raises important questions about the environmental footprint of technology. By embracing sustainable practices and exploring innovative solutions, we can ensure that the future of food is both delicious and environmentally responsible.

19

Chapter 19: The Intersection of Robotics and Culinary Arts

The rise of robotic chefs represents a unique intersection of robotics and culinary arts, where technology meets creativity and tradition. This convergence offers exciting possibilities for innovation and experimentation, transforming the way we approach food and dining. The intersection of robotics and culinary arts is a dynamic and evolving field, where the boundaries of what is possible are constantly being pushed.

One of the most fascinating aspects of this intersection is the fusion of technology and artistic expression. Robotic chefs, equipped with advanced sensors and precision tools, can execute complex techniques and presentation styles that were once the domain of skilled human chefs. This fusion of technology and artistry opens up new possibilities for culinary innovation, allowing chefs to experiment with bold flavors, intricate designs, and cutting-edge cooking methods. The result is a dining experience that is not only delicious but also visually stunning and intellectually stimulating.

Moreover, the integration of robotics into culinary arts offers opportunities for collaboration and interdisciplinary learning. Chefs can work with experts in robotics, AI, and food science to develop new techniques and innovations in the kitchen. This interdisciplinary approach fosters a holistic understanding of the culinary arts, where technology and tradition coexist and complement each other. By promoting collaboration and cross-disciplinary learning, the intersection of robotics and culinary arts is driving the future of culinary innovation.

The presence of robotic chefs in the culinary world also raises important questions about the role of human creativity and intuition. While these machines can replicate recipes with precision, they lack the emotional connection and intuition that human chefs bring to their creations. The dynamic interplay between technology and tradition will shape the future of culinary practices, where both human and robotic chefs contribute their unique strengths to create unforgettable dining experiences.

As we explore the intersection of robotics and culinary arts, it is clear that this convergence offers exciting possibilities for the future. By embracing the potential of robotic chefs while preserving the essence of human creativity and craftsmanship, we can create a culinary landscape that is both innovative and timeless.

20

Chapter 20: The Social Implications of Robotic Chefs

The rise of robotic chefs also has significant social implications, transforming our relationship with food, dining, and each other. As these machines become more integrated into our culinary practices, they are reshaping the way we interact with food and the social dynamics of dining. The social implications of robotic chefs are complex and multifaceted, influencing our perceptions of creativity, tradition, and connection.

One of the most significant social implications of robotic chefs is the potential to democratize gourmet cooking. With these machines, anyone can prepare restaurant-quality meals in the comfort of their own home. This accessibility to high-quality food has the potential to change the way we think about cooking and dining. No longer limited to professional chefs, gourmet cooking is becoming a shared experience that transcends social and economic barriers. This democratization of culinary expertise is transforming the social dynamics of dining, creating new opportunities for connection and engagement.

Moreover, the integration of robotic chefs into our culinary traditions raises questions about the preservation of cultural heritage. Cooking is often seen as a form of artistic expression, deeply rooted in cultural identity and history. The use of robotic chefs challenges the notion of authenticity and tradition in the kitchen. While these machines can replicate recipes with precision, they lack the human touch and intuition that characterize traditional cooking. This tension between technology and tradition will shape the future of culinary practices and our social interactions around food.

The presence of robotic chefs also has the potential to redefine the dining experience itself. In a world where convenience and efficiency are highly valued, robotic chefs offer a new way of experiencing food. Automated kitchens and AI-driven dining experiences are becoming increasingly popular in restaurants and homes. This shift towards automation has the potential to change the way we connect and interact with each other over a meal. The act of sharing a meal, once a deeply communal activity, is being transformed by the presence of robotic chefs.

As we navigate the social landscape shaped by robotic chefs, it is essential to consider the broader implications for society. The integration of technology into our culinary practices challenges our perceptions of creativity, craftsmanship, and authenticity. While robotic chefs offer exciting possibilities for innovation and experimentation, they also raise important questions about the role of human intuition and emotion in the kitchen. The social implications of robotic chefs are a complex and multifaceted phenomenon that will continue to evolve in the coming years.

21

Chapter 21: The Future of Culinary Creativity

As we look to the future of culinary creativity, it is clear that robotic chefs will play a significant role in shaping the culinary landscape. These machines offer exciting possibilities for innovation and experimentation, pushing the boundaries of what is possible in the kitchen. The future of culinary creativity will be defined by the dynamic interplay between technology and tradition, where both human and robotic chefs contribute their unique strengths to create unforgettable dining experiences.

One of the key areas where robotic chefs are driving culinary creativity is in the development of new recipes and techniques. These machines can analyze vast amounts of culinary data, identifying patterns and trends that can inspire new and innovative dishes. By experimenting with new flavors, presentation styles, and cooking methods, robotic chefs can push the boundaries of traditional cooking and create unique culinary experiences. This ability to experiment and innovate is opening up exciting possibilities for culinary creativity.

Moreover, the integration of robotic chefs into the culinary world is fostering a culture of collaboration and interdisciplinary learning. Chefs can work with experts in robotics, AI, and food science to develop new techniques and innovations in the kitchen. This interdisciplinary approach encourages a holistic understanding of the culinary arts, where technology and tradition coexist and complement each other. By promoting collaboration and cross-disciplinary learning, the future of culinary creativity is being shaped by the convergence of technology and artistry.

The presence of robotic chefs also raises important questions about the role of human creativity and intuition. While these machines can replicate recipes with precision, they lack the emotional connection and intuition that human chefs bring to their creations. The dynamic interplay between technology and tradition will shape the future of culinary practices, where both human and robotic chefs contribute their unique strengths to create unforgettable dining experiences. The future of culinary creativity will be defined by the harmonious coexistence of technology and human artistry, offering a new and exciting culinary landscape for generations to come.

As we explore the future of culinary creativity, it is clear that robotic chefs offer exciting possibilities for innovation and experimentation. By embracing the potential of these machines while preserving the essence of human creativity and craftsmanship, we can create a culinary landscape that is both innovative and timeless. The future of culinary creativity is bright, and the dynamic interplay between technology and tradition will continue to drive the evolution of the culinary arts.

22

Chapter 22: The Legacy of Robotic Chefs

As we conclude our exploration of the rise of robotic chefs and their impact on food, society, and the culinary world, it is clear that these machines are leaving a lasting legacy. The integration of technology into our culinary practices offers exciting possibilities for innovation, efficiency, and personalization. However, it also raises important questions about the role of tradition, creativity, and human intuition in the kitchen.

The legacy of robotic chefs is not just about technological advancements but also about the broader implications for our relationship with food and dining. These machines are transforming the way we approach cooking and dining, offering new possibilities for culinary creativity and experimentation. The dynamic interplay between technology and tradition will shape the future of culinary practices, where both human and robotic chefs contribute their unique strengths to create unforgettable dining experiences.

Moreover, the legacy of robotic chefs extends to the broader implications for society and the environment. These machines have the potential to address pressing challenges faced by the food industry, from sustainability and resource optimization to food safety and accessibility.

Taste of the Future: Exploring Food, Society, and the Rise of Robotic Chefs

Discover the transformative journey of robotic chefs as they revolutionize kitchens around the world. From their technological origins to their profound impact on food culture, this book delves into the science, ethics, and social implications of automated cooking. Explore how these mechanical marvels are reshaping culinary education, healthcare, and even space missions. As robotic chefs push the boundaries of culinary creativity and sustainability, they challenge our perceptions of tradition, creativity, and the future of dining. Join us in examining the dynamic interplay between technology and human artistry in this exciting new era of gastronomy.

www.ingramcontent.com/pod-product-compliance
Lightning Source LLC
LaVergne TN
LVHW012130070526
838202LV00056B/5941